Messenger Marketing

B. Vincent

Published by RWG Publishing, 2021.

MESSENGER MARKETING

First edition. August 9, 2021.

Written by B. Vincent.

Also by B. Vincent

Affiliate Marketing
Affiliate Marketing
Affiliate Marketing

Standalone
Business Employee Discipline
Affiliate Recruiting
Business Layoffs & Firings
Business and Entrepreneur Guide
Business Remote Workforce
Career Transition
Project Management
Precision Targeting
Professional Development
Strategic Planning
Content Marketing
Imminent List Building
Getting Past GateKeepers
Banner Ads

Bookkeeping
Bridge Pages
Business Acquisition
Business Bogging
Marketing Automation
Better Meetings
Conversion Optimization
Creative Solutions
Employee Recruitment
Startup Capital
Employee Mentoring
Followership
Servant Leadership
Human Resources
Team Building
Freelancing
Funnel Building
Geo Targeting
Goal Setting
Immanent List Building
Lead Generation
Leadership Course
Leadership Transition
LinkedIn Ads
LinkedIn Marketing
Messenger Marketing
New Management

Table of Contents

Messenger Marketing

Welcome to this seminar on courier advertising. In this course, we will cover how to expand your span with courier bots. This course is partitioned into three modules. Module One covers making and interfacing your little visit account. Module Two, gives us an outline of the smaller than normal talk stage and module three covers setting up your first transmission. When this course is finished, you'll realize how to successfully utilize courier bots for your business. So, moving along, how about we jump into the principal module. OK, folks, welcome to Module One. What's more, this module, our master will cover making and associating your small-scale visit account. So, prepare to take a few notes and we should directly hop in.

Module One

Alright, folks, so how about we begin with setting up a little visit account. In the first place, go to the smaller than usual visit site, then, at that point click the Get Started free catch. Then, at that point sign in with Facebook and allow little talk to get to and deal with your page. If it's not too much trouble, note that small talk just works for a Facebook page and not for individual Facebook account. Since you have associated your Facebook page to small visit, the dashboard should resemble this. Presently how about we set up our hello message. on the dashboard, click the settings as an afterthought menu. Then, at that point, type in your hello text inside the textbox. The hello text is utilized to portray your business or let guests know how your courier bot can help them. You are restricted to 160 characters, yet you can add emoticons to make it seriously inviting. When your content with your hello message, click safe. To review your hello text, click the connection that sees perceive what it looks like. A spring up will show up and you'll perceive what it looks like on a portable screen. Make sure to consistently watch that it looks great on the portable screen in light of the fact that a ton of your clients will associate with your page utilizing their telephones. Presently we should set up the welcome message. Go to mechanization as an afterthought menu, then, at that point click invite message. It ought to be the third one from the alternatives. This is the way the arrangement page resembles. At the top bar you have the choice to incapacitate and empower the welcome message. You have the alternative to see and distribute it. And afterward the three spots what and toward the end is for the alternatives, for example, rename, copy, duplicate to another page, erase, and return to distribute.

We haven't distributed our welcome message at this point so supporters can't see anything on their end. Presently we should add our welcome message. Type your welcome message in the content box. How about we add a placeholder to customize the message. To do this snap anyplace inside the case. Then, at that point select the second symbol from the dark bar that shows up. It seems as though two wavy sections with a spot inside. Ensure your cursor is in the right area inside the textbox. Snap the placeholder that you like to utilize, and you'll see it seem featured in blue. So, make your welcome message amicable. We should add emoticons. Snap anyplace inside the content box once more. Then, at that point select the smiley symbol and the dark bar. Snap the emoticon that you like to utilize, and it ought to show up in your message. Here are some well-known emoticons that you can utilize. The message naturally saves in a review ought to be noticeable on the portable screen on the right. Once done, click Publish at the upper right corner. This is the message your endorsers will check whether they click the Get Started button or sends you a directive interestingly. Presently how about we set up our default answer. Go to mechanization once more, then, at that point click default answer. It ought to be the second one from the alternatives. You should see a layout message inside the content box. You can supplant this message then, at that point click anyplace outside the content box to save it.

The default answer is sent when the board doesn't have the foggiest idea what to reply. For instance, in case there are no watchword matches, you can propose your clients to type a catchphrase or give them a menu. Then, how about we figure out how to utilize catchphrases. Go to computerization, then, at that point click watchwords. It ought to be the fourth one from the alternatives. Watchwords are utilized to computerize your board answers when a client asks something. This is valuable for generally posed inquiries. broaden on this page is the dynamic and latent flip switch. This shows which rule is right now being utilized. Next is the standard. The two default ones are the buy in and withdraw rule. At the point when a client sends the watchword begin or buy in, they will get this buy in to what exactly message as an answer. Then, at that point as an extra activity, they will be bought in to your bot.

The subsequent one is the withdraw rule. At the point when the client sends the watchword stop or withdraw, they will get the withdraw from the blog message. Also, no activity is important to be set since they have as of now withdrew. Presently we should add our own catchphrase. Snap the Add new catchphrase at the upper right corner. Then, at that point type the catchphrase you need to utilize. Then, at that point click Create catchphrase. Then, we should set up our computerized answer. Snap Create new answer to make another message or select a current one from the premade layouts. Then, at that point click select this stream. Assuming you need to change the standard, simply click message is and you'll see the accessible guideline. message is just acknowledging watchword that are by and large determined. This standard is extremely severe. It's not case delicate, however in the event that there are extra letters, spaces, or images, answer your activities won't be set off. Message contains is more adaptable. It can perceive watchword in sentences. Simply be cautious utilizing short watchwords that can be confused with the genuine catchphrase that you need. At long last, you can likewise put extra activity by choosing starting from the drop menu when you click the Add activity. Assuming you need to erase a current guideline, click the been on the right side.

Module Two

Hello people, welcome to Module Two. In this module, our master will give us an outline of the smaller than usual talk stage. So, prepare to take a few notes and we should directly bounce in.

Okay folks, so we should do a speedy outline of the smaller than normal talk stage. Smaller than normal visit is a help that permits you to make talk bots for Facebook Messenger. A visit bot or a bot is a progression of robotized discussions that get answer normal inquiries from your clients. This could be to clarify what your items or administrations are. You can likewise utilize it to assemble data about your clients and support them towards a deal. Presently we should do a speedy visit through the scaled down talk dashboard. On the left side, you'll see the menu. The first on the menu is the dashboard. This is the place where you'll see the general insights of your endorsers and unsubscribers. You'll likewise see here the connection to your bot. At whatever point your client access this connection, they will be diverted to your courier. Next is the beginning advance. This is the place where you'll see the profile of your supporters. On the right are the rundown sifted by an apparatus every client selected in or bought in to. We have the labels, gadgets, arrangements, and promotions. Then, how about we go to the live visit. This instrument permits you to speak with your endorsers in a single spot. Since we can associate the board to different channels like Facebook Messenger, SMS, and email. We can have discussions with every one of our clients through the live visit. Then, we should discuss development instruments.

This is the place where you can set up a gadget or an advertisement to assist you with bringing endorsers into your bot. Next, we have broadcasting this is like a message stream. This can comprise of one message, or a few messages connected together. Furthermore, under this instrument are communicates and paid messages. Next is the robotization. This is the place where we set up the programmed answers dependent on our client's association with our bot. We have the fundamental menu. This is the place where we can set up and propose choices for our crowd. The default answer where we can set up customized reaction when the bot doesn't have the foggiest idea what to reply. Next is the welcome message or the message that they see subsequent to buying in. Next is the watchwords where we alter answers dependent on catchphrases utilized by our clients. We likewise have the groupings.

It's a smaller than usual talk highlight that permits you to buy in clients from your starting points to the chain of messages that can be isolated by deferrals of various legs. The last one is the standards. This is the place where you can set up a trigger. Furthermore, when it occurs, the board needs to perform explicit activities or activity. Presently we should discuss the scaled down visit stream or Flow Builder. Consider it a visual guide of the multitude of messages activities and changes between them. It gives you a 10,000-foot perspective of the entire collaboration without exchanging between single messages. Presently we should do an outline of the primary board settings. At the overall wound you'll initially see the hello text segment. This is the message your client will see before they start a collaboration with your bot. This might be a concise depiction or a lead test to make your future endorsers message your page. Next is the card URL shortener. This element requires an ace membership, and this records your messages, CTR or active clicking factor information. Then, we have the blog time zone. All sent out information will be founded on the time zone that you have set here.

Then, we have the clone to another page. This exchanges all substance of your board to another page. This is valuable assuming you need to reuse a portion of the substance that you have effectively made. Next, we have the invigorate Facebook consents. Courier stage can surprise the drop page consent or administrator secret phrase change. If there should arise an occurrence of any issue with content sending or administration arrangement, you can utilize this revive authorization to acquire a smooth access once more. Then, at that point we have console input, you might cripple console contribution to make the tireless menu The lone way for an individual to interface with your courier bot. Then, at that point we have beginnings perceivability. This conceals all erased and withdraw clients in crowd. Finally, we have the cripple bot for this page. This element detaches little visit from your Facebook page, it doesn't erase any substance or endorsers. Also, you can undoubtedly get entrance again by interfacing your Facebook to small scale visit to get Don't neglect to drop dynamic ace membership first prior to handicapping the bot. Presently we should discuss the live talk tab, you can pick between two live visit practices. The main alternative beginnings a live visit meeting with any messages from a client.

The subsequent one requires a catch or a fast answer before it begins a live talk meeting. Then, at that point we have personas in live visit. This is for a more customized discussions with your client. This permits your clients to see the name and profile image of the specialist that they are conversing with. Then, at that point we have shut every single open discussion. This permits you to check all open discussions is finished. Next, we have the sound notices. This empowers or handicaps in application sound alarms. In conclusion, we have this piece. This permits you to make canned reactions and send them in a live visit discussion in a single tick. Presently on to the development Tools tab. First, we have the gadget confinement. This confines your gadgets by picking a language from the rundown. English us is the picked language as a matter of course. approve site permits you to add sites to your approved rundown. Next, we have marking. Here you can wind down smaller than expected talk marking in embeddable gadgets, overlay gadgets, and point of arrival development devices. How about we currently go to the Notifications tab. The main area is the email address where warnings will be sent. Then, we have the recurrence of the endorsers report. You can pick every day, week by week or month to month. Then, at that point we have live visit notices.

This empowers or impairs a scope of live talk warnings to help you support your crowd and track leads. The tell progressed activity is empowered assuming you need to get warnings when a client performs at explicit activity in your transmissions, welcome messages, pick in messages, etc. Finally, we have the courier warnings up into your bot to have the option to get bot notices in courier and to review bot content. We should now go to custom fields. Custom Fields permits you to make custom fields which can store any data about your supporters. Then again, purchased fields permits you to store your what information and set the qualities relying upon your endorser's activities. They appear as though custom client fields yet can store esteems which are identified with your purchased, for instance, text, numbers and recipes date and time. Up next is the labels tab. Here you can make new labels and erase the ones you at this point don't require. A tag is an approach to portion your endorsers, you can add and eliminate labels from clients to demonstrate that they are a section or not a piece of a specific gathering. We presently go to the Users tab. Here you can deal with the administrators of your smaller than usual visit account. All Users who approach a specific bot inside smaller than usual visit one of four client jobs that characterize which segments of the little talk are accessible to them and can be changed. Then, at that point we have the installments tab. What's more, this tab, you can associate stripe account, select cash type for your Buy button and select installments warning sort. request history for everything buys can likewise be found here. Next, we have the reconciliation step, you'll have the option to set up outsider incorporations utilizing this tab.

Next is the SMS showcasing tab. This tab is for keeping drawn in with individuals who have communicated interest in your image utilizing SMS. Kindly know that it is as of now accessible in the US market as it were. Next is the email promoting tab. Like SMS promoting. This is to keep your supporters connected with utilizing the email channel. The subsequent stage is for building. This tab deals with your membership, you can drop or update your membership through this tab. Up next is the API tab. Here you're ready to produce a token to begin utilizing smaller than normal visit API. The subsequent stage is the introduced formats. Under this tab, you will track down every one of the formats that are introduced to your page. Here you can see the substance of the layouts and furthermore modify a portion of its boundaries like location, telephone number, etc.

At long last, we have the logs tab. In this part, you can check whether there are any issues with your bots working. Inside the logs, you will discover a rundown of blunders and fixes as they happen. At the point when the issue is fixed, you'll see a positive outcome note in the logs. Presently we should discuss layouts. Layouts are fundamentally a pre-planned board structure that you can utilize so you don't need to begin without any preparation to do your message and activity streams. You can choose from any highlighted formats here. Peruse the about area, and snap Install when you're prepared. The second to the keep going on our menu is the My Profile page. This is the place where you can add a Facebook page that you oversee, or you need to change to. What's more, you can likewise make your own format. The last advance is the place where you can create your API toolbox. Presently on the off chance that you need extra data, you can basically tap the Help connect at the base. You can choose to peruse the documentation, watch the video instructional exercises, enlist an office, present a ticket, or perhaps join the small visit local area.

Module Three

Okay, welcome to Module Three. In this module, our master will tell us the best way to set up our first transmission. So, prepare to take a few notes and how about we directly bounce in.

Alright, so we should begin with setting up our first transmission. Go to broadcasting on your menu, then, at that point click add new transmission at the upper right corner. Then, at that point select courier. On the right side you can change to essential developer or the Flow Builder. How about we use Flow Builder to have a superior visual of our transmission stream. Snap beginning advance and a sidebar will consequently show up. So, like different resources Our substance type for this model then, at that point, how about we type in our message. The message should peruse Hey, their first name, get my free multi day Christmas Fitness Bootcamp series. Is it true that you are intrigued? Then, at that point we should add the two choices. Indeed, I'm intrigued and pass.

Presently how about we interface our alternatives to an activity. drag your mouse from the main alternative and afterward select Start stream. Snap to choose a stream then, at that point browse your premade layouts. Then, at that point click select this stream. We should do likewise for the subsequent choice, however this time we'll pick send message. Then, at that point how about we add a catch. Find out additional. Presently how about we interface the catches a similar stream. Whenever everything is said the following stage is for our transmission Settings. Select the substance type. We have three choices here, non-limited time or blended substance. Next is the limited time content as it were. And afterward we have the subsequent kind. Recollect that the transmission choices are dependent upon the Facebook Messenger stage strategy. To try not to get suspended, we need to follow this then we have focused on, you can focus on every one of your transmissions by the accompanying conditions. select from the rundown beneath. Then, we have booked transmissions, begin sending your transmission quickly or plan it to be sent on a specific date and time.

Then, we have time zone settings send all simultaneously conveys your transmission right away. Use time travel to plan time as indicated by your endorsers time zone. Furthermore, in conclusion, use limits finishing time to send message at the earliest opportunity once clients daytime in the screen time zone matches wanted conveyance hours. Presently we go to the warning settings. This just applies to versatile warnings. Ordinary pop-up message will make a sound and show a telephone warning. Just a single standard warning triggers just a single ordinary notice and the rest will be in quiet mode. Just two normal warning triggers just two ordinary notices and the rest will be in quiet mode. Quiet push will show a telephone warning without a sound and quiet transmission won't show any notice whatsoever. When your content with the arrangement, click Send now or timetable message at the upper right corner. Presently we should find out about the smaller than usual visit groupings. The arrangement is a component that permits supporters of get chain of message at a given timeframe.

We can begin by going to robotization on the menu, then, at that point pick groupings. Then, at that point, click the add new succession at the upper right. Type a name for your succession and afterward click Create. You'll naturally see the premade message formats, you can change the succession send time by tapping on the timetable then, at that point pick another date or time you like. On the off chance that you need to add another message to your grouping simply click the Add message button. On the right you'll likewise see the examination of your grouping sent discloses to you the quantity of clients that accepted your message. clicks discloses to you the quantity of clients who click the catch and your message. What's more, the last two are the calculations for your open rate and your active clicking factor. Presently we should discuss streams. Furthermore, the sidebar when you soon after the robotization rules, you'll discover a streams envelope. Stream Builder is a visual editorial manager, all things considered, activities and advances between them. We should have a speedy outline of the stream supervisors' components. At the top you'll discover a pursuit bar to look through streams by a name. Next, we have the add new stream button. We likewise have the switch see. Snap flip View catch to switch among records and thumbnails. Then, at that point we have the envelopes to assist you with getting sorted out your streams. Next, we have the brilliant organizers to store your present mechanization Under center you'll see your stream data which contains the name the channels of your stream, the quantity of runs and when it was adjusted. The three dabs on the right open the setting menu that permits you to perform activities. Rename changes the stream name, copy clones your stream to a similar organizer. We additionally have the offer this stream, duplicate to another page, and erase which moves your stream to the waste.

Don't miss out!

Visit the website below and you can sign up to receive emails whenever B. Vincent publishes a new book. There's no charge and no obligation.

https://books2read.com/r/B-A-QWUO-HICRB

BOOKS 2 READ

Connecting independent readers to independent writers.

Also by B. Vincent

Affiliate Marketing
Affiliate Marketing
Affiliate Marketing

Standalone
Business Employee Discipline
Affiliate Recruiting
Business Layoffs & Firings
Business and Entrepreneur Guide
Business Remote Workforce
Career Transition
Project Management
Precision Targeting
Professional Development
Strategic Planning
Content Marketing
Imminent List Building
Getting Past GateKeepers
Banner Ads

Bookkeeping
Bridge Pages
Business Acquisition
Business Bogging
Marketing Automation
Better Meetings
Conversion Optimization
Creative Solutions
Employee Recruitment
Startup Capital
Employee Mentoring
Followership
Servant Leadership
Human Resources
Team Building
Freelancing
Funnel Building
Geo Targeting
Goal Setting
Immanent List Building
Lead Generation
Leadership Course
Leadership Transition
LinkedIn Ads
LinkedIn Marketing
Messenger Marketing
New Management

About the Publisher

Accepting manuscripts in the most categories. We love to help people get their words available to the world.

Revival Waves of Glory focus is to provide more options to be published. We do traditional paperbacks, hardcovers, audio books and ebooks all over the world. A traditional royalty-based publisher that offers self-publishing options, Revival Waves provides a very author friendly and transparent publishing process, with President Bill Vincent involved in the full process of your book. Send us your manuscript and we will contact you as soon as possible.

Contact: Bill Vincent at rwgpublishing@yahoo.com www.rwgpublishing.com